My Journal

Be Present

Beauty

Be in nature ... or visualize

In a forest. A tree. A plant. Describe.
_____
_____

Observe a leaf. Color? Dry? Alive?
_____
_____

The air. Misty? Warm? Raindrops?
_____
_____

The smell. Describe.
_____
_____

Be still … Be present in this moment

Breathe

Take a deep breath & write …

Week 1: Presence

Monday_____
_____
_____

Tuesday_____
_____
_____

Wednesday_____
_____
_____

Thursday_____
_____
_____

Friday_____
_____
_____

Saturday_____
_____
_____

Sunday_____
_____
_____

Practice living in the moment

Week 2: Mindfulness

Monday_____
_____
_____

Tuesday_____
_____
_____

Wednesday_____
_____
_____

Thursday_____
_____
_____

Friday_____
_____
_____

Saturday_____
_____
_____

Sunday_____
_____
_____

See the beauty that surrounds you

Week 3: Pursuit

Monday_____
_____
_____

Tuesday_____
_____
_____

Wednesday_____
_____
_____

Thursday_____
_____
_____

Friday_____
_____
_____

Saturday_____
_____
_____

Sunday_____
_____
_____

You've got this!

Authenticity
Living my own truth

3. _____
_____
_____
_____
4. _____
_____
_____
_____
_____

I am real

3 times I was NOT able to express my feelings clearly. No self-judgement.

1. _____
_____
_____
_____
2. _____
_____
_____
_____
3. _____
_____
_____
_____
4. _____
_____
_____
_____

4 lessons I have learned from mistakes

1. _____
_____
_____
_____
2. _____
_____
_____
_____

Reveal my truth

3 times I was able to express my emotions freely with clarity

1. _____

2. _____

3. _____

Notes

Week 4: Truthfulness

Monday_____
_____
_____

Tuesday_____
_____
_____

Wednesday_____
_____
_____

Thursday_____
_____
_____

Friday_____
_____
_____

Saturday_____
_____
_____

Sunday_____
_____
_____

Just be you

Week 5: Genuineness

Monday _____
_____
_____

Tuesday _____
_____
_____

Wednesday _____
_____
_____

Thursday _____
_____
_____

Friday _____
_____
_____

Saturday _____
_____
_____

Sunday _____
_____
_____

Being genuine can mean being vulnerable

Week 6: Courage

Monday _____
_____
_____

Tuesday _____
_____
_____

Wednesday _____
_____
_____

Thursday _____
_____
_____

Friday _____
_____
_____

Saturday _____
_____
_____

Sunday _____
_____
_____

Be awesome!

Be Happy

Life is good when

1. _____
2. _____
3. _____
4. _____
5. _____
6. _____

Favorite Things

8 things that make me smile

1. _____
2. _____
3. _____
4. _____
5. _____
6. _____
7. _____
8. _____

Cats Raindrops Coffee Friends Hummingbirds

Draw in the Box ...
Well-Loved Things

Uplifting

4 heartwarming stories I've lived, heard or read. Smile!

1. _____

2. _____

3. _____

4. _____

Notes

Week 7: Happiness

Monday_____
_____
_____

Tuesday_____
_____
_____

Wednesday_____
_____
_____

Thursday_____
_____
_____

Friday_____
_____
_____

Saturday_____
_____
_____

Sunday_____
_____
_____

Seize the day!

Week 8: Love

Monday _____
_____
_____

Tuesday _____
_____
_____

Wednesday _____
_____
_____

Thursday _____
_____
_____

Friday _____
_____
_____

Saturday _____
_____
_____

Sunday _____
_____
_____

Count your blessings

Week 9: Trust

Monday_____
_____
_____

Tuesday_____
_____
_____

Wednesday_____
_____
_____

Thursday_____
_____
_____

Friday_____
_____
_____

Saturday_____
_____
_____

Sunday_____
_____
_____

Be brave

Past Memories

6 dearest childhood memories

1. _____
2. _____
3. _____
4. _____
5. _____
6. _____

I remember when ...

3 perfect days from my childhood

1. _____
_____
_____
_____

2. _____
_____
_____
_____

3. _____
_____
_____
_____

Cherish

3 big lessons I learned as a child

1. _____

2. _____

3. _____

I am a child again. I write in my diary ...

Week 10: Reminisce

Monday _____
_____
_____

Tuesday _____
_____
_____

Wednesday _____
_____
_____

Thursday _____
_____
_____

Friday _____
_____
_____

Saturday _____
_____
_____

Sunday _____
_____
_____

Recall experiences long past with a sense of nostalgia

Week 11: Thoughtfulness

Monday _____
_____
_____

Tuesday _____
_____
_____

Wednesday _____
_____
_____

Thursday _____
_____
_____

Friday _____
_____
_____

Saturday _____
_____
_____

Sunday _____
_____
_____

Find your balance

Week 12: Resilience

Monday _____
_____
_____

Tuesday _____
_____
_____

Wednesday _____
_____
_____

Thursday _____
_____
_____

Friday _____
_____
_____

Saturday _____
_____
_____

Sunday _____
_____
_____

Never give up

Respect
Appreciate yourself

I respect myself by respecting others. 4 feelings I experienced when fully respecting someone.

1. _____
2. _____
3. _____
4. _____

Look in the mirror & completely respect yourself

3 times I did or did not have much patience with someone. No self-judgement.

1. _____
2. _____
3. _____

Patience

3 ways I can improve having respect for myself and others

1. _____

2. _____

3. _____

Notes

Week 13: Admiration

Monday _____
_____
_____

Tuesday _____
_____
_____

Wednesday _____
_____
_____

Thursday _____
_____
_____

Friday _____
_____
_____

Saturday _____
_____
_____

Sunday _____
_____
_____

Give respect to receive respect

Week 14: Boundaries

Monday_____
_____
_____

Tuesday_____
_____
_____

Wednesday_____
_____
_____

Thursday_____
_____
_____

Friday_____
_____
_____

Saturday_____
_____
_____

Sunday_____
_____
_____

Other people don't define your boundaries

Week 15: Believe

Monday_____
_____
_____

Tuesday_____
_____
_____

Wednesday_____
_____
_____

Thursday_____
_____
_____

Friday_____
_____
_____

Saturday_____
_____
_____

Sunday_____
_____
_____

Don't stop believing

Coping With Past Memories

I remember when...

Painful experiences that made me a stronger person. Negative memories that have a thread of positivity running through them.

1. _____
2. _____

3. _____

Anguish

Gently remember 3 difficult days as a child. Rewrite those days into good ones.

1. _____
2. _____
3. _____

I am a child again. I
write in my diary ...

Week 16: Healing

Monday _____
_____
_____

Tuesday _____
_____
_____

Wednesday _____
_____
_____

Thursday _____
_____
_____

Friday _____
_____
_____

Saturday _____
_____
_____

Sunday _____
_____
_____

The avoidance of pain increases it. To heal, you must walk through the doorway of grief.

Week 17: Reflection

Monday _____
_____
_____

Tuesday _____
_____
_____

Wednesday _____
_____
_____

Thursday _____
_____
_____

Friday _____
_____
_____

Saturday _____
_____
_____

Sunday _____
_____
_____

Take a break from pain. Read. Socialize. Take a bubble bath.

Week 18: Care

Monday_____
_____
_____

Tuesday_____
_____
_____

Wednesday_____
_____
_____

Thursday_____
_____
_____

Friday_____
_____
_____

Saturday_____
_____
_____

Sunday_____
_____
_____

Take care of yourself first

Affirmations

I am worthy of love

I carry strength, courage, and resilience within me

I have the ability to overcome any challenge life gives me

Self-esteem

Self-esteem combined with confidence is one of the key hallmarks of success.

I will continue to learn and grow

I love the person I am becoming

I deserve the love I am given

I release my negative thoughts and embrace positivity

Mistakes are a stepping stone to success. They are the path I must tread to achieve my dreams

Write in a box ... affirmation

Accomplishments + Self-Esteem = Increased Happiness

2 of my biggest accomplishments

1. _____
   _____
   _____
2. _____
   _____
   _____

Week 19: Success

Monday_____

Tuesday_____

Wednesday_____

Thursday_____

Friday_____

Saturday_____

Sunday_____

Week 20: Dream

Monday_____
_____
_____
_____
_____
_____
_____

Tuesday_____
_____
_____
_____
_____
_____
_____

Wednesday_____
_____
_____
_____
_____
_____
_____

Thursday_____
_____
_____
_____
_____
_____
_____

Friday_____
_____
_____
_____
_____
_____
_____

Saturday_____
_____
_____
_____
_____
_____
_____

Sunday_____
_____
_____
_____
_____
_____
_____

Week 21: Discover

Monday_____

Tuesday_____

Wednesday_____

Thursday_____

Friday_____

Saturday_____

Sunday_____

Maturity
Personal Growth

3. _____

Strength

3 times I did not succeed. No self-judgement.

1. _____

2. _____

3. _____

3 things I am striving for

1. _____

2. _____

I am strong

Rewrite those 3 experiences into success stories. Feel it!

1. _____
   _____
   _____

2. _____
   _____
   _____

3. _____
   _____
   _____

Notes

Week 22: Blossoming

Monday_____
_____
_____

Tuesday_____
_____
_____

Wednesday_____
_____
_____

Thursday_____
_____
_____

Friday_____
_____
_____

Saturday_____
_____
_____

Sunday_____
_____
_____

Week 23: Growth

Monday_____
_____
_____

Tuesday_____
_____
_____

Wednesday_____
_____
_____

Thursday_____
_____
_____

Friday_____
_____
_____

Saturday_____
_____
_____

Sunday_____
_____
_____

Week 24: Experience

Monday_____
_____
_____

Tuesday_____
_____
_____

Wednesday_____
_____
_____

Thursday_____
_____
_____

Friday_____
_____
_____

Saturday_____
_____
_____

Sunday_____
_____
_____

With affirmations floating around in my head, I color …

Week 25: Journey

Monday _____
_____
_____

Tuesday _____
_____
_____

Wednesday _____
_____
_____

Thursday _____
_____
_____

Friday _____
_____
_____

Saturday _____
_____
_____

Sunday _____
_____
_____

Journey far and wide

Week 26: Creativity

Monday _____
_____
_____

Tuesday _____
_____
_____

Wednesday _____
_____
_____

Thursday _____
_____
_____

Friday _____
_____
_____

Saturday _____
_____
_____

Sunday _____
_____
_____

Enjoy your own company

Week 27: Playful

Monday _____
_____
_____

Tuesday _____
_____
_____

Wednesday _____
_____
_____

Thursday _____
_____
_____

Friday _____
_____
_____

Saturday _____
_____
_____

Sunday _____
_____
_____

Inspire and awaken your heart

Gratitude

3 things I am grateful for right now

1. _____
   _____
   _____
   _____

2. _____
   _____
   _____
   _____

3. _____
   _____
   _____
   _____

Being Thankful

2 activities that bring me joy

1. _____
   _____
   _____
   _____

2. _____
   _____
   _____
   _____

3. _____
   _____
   _____
   _____

Places I Love

Favorite space in my home
_____

Why? Describe
_____
_____
_____
_____

Favorite place in my town or city
_____

Why? Describe
_____
_____
_____
_____

Be free! Doodle a flower.

Week 28: Thank You

Monday _____
_____
_____

Tuesday _____
_____
_____

Wednesday _____
_____
_____

Thursday _____
_____
_____

Friday _____
_____
_____

Saturday _____
_____
_____

Sunday _____
_____
_____

Stop and smell the roses

Week 29: Blessed

Monday_____
_____
_____

Tuesday_____
_____
_____

Wednesday_____
_____
_____

Thursday_____
_____
_____

Friday_____
_____
_____

Saturday_____
_____
_____

Sunday_____
_____
_____

Don't quit your daydream

Week 30: Celebrate

Monday_____
_____
_____

Tuesday_____
_____
_____

Wednesday_____
_____
_____

Thursday_____
_____
_____

Friday_____
_____
_____

Saturday_____
_____
_____

Sunday_____
_____
_____

Kindness changes everything

Self-Confidence
Forgive yourself

3. _____
4. _____

Get naked. Look in the mirror & completely love yourself

4 of my amazing talents

1. _____
2. _____
3. _____
4. _____

Release

4 things that convey negativity. Get rid of them.

1. _____
2. _____

4 experiences that affected my self-confidence. Describe.

1. _____

2. _____

3. _____

4. _____

Notes

Week 31: Struggle

Monday_____
_____
_____

Tuesday_____
_____
_____

Wednesday_____
_____
_____

Thursday_____
_____
_____

Friday_____
_____
_____

Saturday_____
_____
_____

Sunday_____
_____
_____

Let it be

Week 32: Reality

Monday _____
_____
_____

Tuesday _____
_____
_____

Wednesday _____
_____
_____

Thursday _____
_____
_____

Friday _____
_____
_____

Saturday _____
_____
_____

Sunday _____
_____
_____

You will find your way

Week 33: Attitude

Monday _____
_____
_____

Tuesday _____
_____
_____

Wednesday _____
_____
_____

Thursday _____
_____
_____

Friday _____
_____
_____

Saturday _____
_____
_____

Sunday _____
_____
_____

Small steps every day

More Gratitude

3 body parts I am most grateful for today … nose to smell a rose

1. _____
   _____
   _____

2. _____
   _____
   _____

3. _____
   _____
   _____

Joy

3 things I take for granted … clean water, food

1. _____
   _____
   _____

2. _____
   _____
   _____

3. _____
   _____
   _____

Places I Love

Favorite space in the world
_____

Why? Describe
_____
_____
_____
_____

Favorite town or city in the world
_____

Why? Describe
_____
_____
_____
_____

Be free! Doodle a donkey!

Week 34: Peace

Monday_____

Tuesday_____

Wednesday_____

Thursday_____

Friday_____

Saturday_____

Sunday_____

Devote yourself to an idea

Week 35: Overcome

Monday _____
_____
_____

Tuesday _____
_____
_____

Wednesday _____
_____
_____

Thursday _____
_____
_____

Friday _____
_____
_____

Saturday _____
_____
_____

Sunday _____
_____
_____

The only constant in life in change

Week 36: Enjoy

Monday

Tuesday

Wednesday

Thursday

Friday

Saturday

Sunday

Have no fear

A Creative Meditation

Psychologist Carl Jung believed that coloring mandalas helped his patients experience benefits similar to meditation, such as inner calm, stress reduction, and enhanced self-awareness.

Week 37: Perspective

Monday_____

_____
_____
_____
_____
_____
_____
_____

Tuesday_____

_____
_____
_____
_____
_____
_____
_____

Wednesday_____

_____
_____
_____
_____
_____
_____
_____

Thursday_____

_____
_____
_____
_____
_____
_____
_____

Friday_____

_____
_____
_____
_____
_____
_____
_____

Saturday_____

_____
_____
_____
_____
_____
_____
_____

Sunday_____

_____
_____
_____
_____
_____
_____
_____

Week 38: Expression

Monday_____

_____
_____
_____
_____
_____
_____

Tuesday_____

_____
_____
_____
_____
_____
_____

Wednesday_____

_____
_____
_____
_____
_____
_____

Thursday_____

_____
_____
_____
_____
_____
_____

Friday_____

_____
_____
_____
_____
_____
_____

Saturday_____

_____
_____
_____
_____
_____
_____

Sunday_____

_____
_____
_____
_____
_____

Week 39: Embrace

Monday_____

Tuesday_____

Wednesday_____

Thursday_____

Friday_____

Saturday_____

Sunday_____

Accomplishment

Tough things I did that led to personal accomplishments

1. _____
2. _____
3. _____
4. _____

2. _____
3. _____
4. _____

Achievement

4 times when I procrastinated on a task that ended up being easier than I thought it would be

1. _____

Write in the box ... most satisfying accomplishment

Desire

4 skills I have that most people don't possess

1. _____

2. _____

3. _____

4. _____

Notes

Week 40: Experience

Monday _____
_____
_____

Tuesday _____
_____
_____

Wednesday _____
_____
_____

Thursday _____
_____
_____

Friday _____
_____
_____

Saturday _____
_____
_____

Sunday _____
_____
_____

Week 41: Forgive

Monday _____
_____
_____

Tuesday _____
_____
_____

Wednesday _____
_____
_____

Thursday _____
_____
_____

Friday _____
_____
_____

Saturday _____
_____
_____

Sunday _____
_____
_____

Week 42: Imagine

Monday_____
_____
_____

Tuesday_____
_____
_____

Wednesday_____
_____
_____

Thursday_____
_____
_____

Friday_____
_____
_____

Saturday_____
_____
_____

Sunday_____
_____
_____

Self-Care

Nourish...Exercise...Sleep
Relax
Be Social...Have Fun
Intimacy
Take a Bathe...Read a Book

Enjoy it all

4 new self-care practices I'm going to begin

1. _____
   _____
   _____
2. _____
   _____
   _____
3. _____
   _____
   _____
4. _____
   _____
   _____

4 of my favorite self-care practices

1. _____
   _____
   _____
2. _____
   _____
   _____
3. _____
   _____
   _____
4. _____
   _____
   _____

Write in the box...my ultimate self-care practice

Week 43: Serendipity

Monday_____
_____
_____

Tuesday_____
_____
_____

Wednesday_____
_____
_____

Thursday_____
_____
_____

Friday_____
_____
_____

Saturday_____
_____
_____

Sunday_____
_____
_____

Life is short. Live it!

Week 44: Acceptance

Monday _____
_____
_____

Tuesday _____
_____
_____

Wednesday _____
_____
_____

Thursday _____
_____
_____

Friday _____
_____
_____

Saturday _____
_____
_____

Sunday _____
_____
_____

Forgive quickly

Week 45: Shifting

Monday _____
_____
_____

Tuesday _____
_____
_____

Wednesday _____
_____
_____

Thursday _____
_____
_____

Friday _____
_____
_____

Saturday _____
_____
_____

Sunday _____
_____
_____

Replace negative patterns of thinking

More Self-Care

Unplug

Stargaze

Go for a Walk

Pamper yourself

4 ways I create balance and organize my life

1. _____
   _____
   _____
2. _____
   _____
   _____
3. _____
   _____
   _____
4. _____
   _____
   _____

4 ways self-care is helping me to thrive and obtain happiness

1. _____
   _____
   _____
   _____
2. _____
   _____
   _____
   _____
3. _____
   _____
   _____
   _____
4. _____
   _____
   _____
   _____

Get to Know Me

Garden...Sip Tea

Cuddle a Cat...Journal

Unconditionally Love Me

Be free! Doodle a Dandelion!

Week 46: Positivity

Monday _____
_____
_____

Tuesday _____
_____
_____

Wednesday _____
_____
_____

Thursday _____
_____
_____

Friday _____
_____
_____

Saturday _____
_____
_____

Sunday _____
_____
_____

All we have is now

Week 47: Understanding

Monday _____
_____
_____

Tuesday _____
_____
_____

Wednesday _____
_____
_____

Thursday _____
_____
_____

Friday _____
_____
_____

Saturday _____
_____
_____

Sunday _____
_____
_____

Life is what you make it

Week 48: Intuition

Monday ___

Tuesday ___

Wednesday ___

Thursday ___

Friday ___

Saturday ___

Sunday ___

If not now, when

Walking Meditation and Color Art
(Indoors? Visualize as you color)

Walk ... Be One With Nature. Does the air smell like evergreens? Are you tasting berries picked from a bush? Do you hear a bird call?

Week 49: Shifting

Monday _____
_____
_____

Tuesday _____
_____
_____

Wednesday _____
_____
_____

Thursday _____
_____
_____

Friday _____
_____
_____

Saturday _____
_____
_____

Sunday _____
_____
_____

Self-care feeds my spiritual self

Week 50: Awareness

Monday_____
_____
_____

Tuesday_____
_____
_____

Wednesday_____
_____
_____

Thursday_____
_____
_____

Friday_____
_____
_____

Saturday_____
_____
_____

Sunday_____
_____
_____

You are enough

Week 51: Intention

Monday _____
_____
_____

Tuesday _____
_____
_____

Wednesday _____
_____
_____

Thursday _____
_____
_____

Friday _____
_____
_____

Saturday _____
_____
_____

Sunday _____
_____
_____

Make your own sunshine

Week 52: Completion

Monday _____

Tuesday _____

Wednesday _____

Thursday _____

Friday _____

Saturday _____

Sunday _____

Nothing worth having comes easy

Journal Reflection - What I have realized ...

Questions or Comments? Email: MayaKealohaBooks@gmail.com

www.ingramcontent.com/pod-product-compliance
Lightning Source LLC
Chambersburg PA
CBHW081015040426
42444CB00014B/3211